Behold

CHRISTI GEE

A CHRISTMAS ADVENT JOURNEY

ADDITIONAL RESOURCES
FOR YOUR JOURNEY AT:

BeholdAdvent.com

Behold: A Christmas Advent Journey

Published by Christi Gee
Printed in the United States of America

ISBN: 978-1979767811

All emphasis in Scripture quotations has been added by the author.

To my baby,
who loves Advent more
than any person I know.
Through your eyes,
it takes on a whole new meaning.
May you never lose the wonder.

Contents

Grace appearing. Glory premiering.
God overshadowing.

Promises fulfilled. Hope that thrills.
Peace and goodwill.

One who broke through the darkness,
breaks our chains,
and knows our weakness.

Behold!
He came. He abides. He comes.

Foreword

I have to confess. I haven't been a big Advent person in the past. My daughter is the one who goes crazy over this seasonal opportunity.

Me? I usually have too much to do. Hellooooo? Mom, here. The one responsible for decorating, list-making, gift-buying, cookie-baking, church-volunteering, program-coordinating … you get the idea.

So, when she had the idea for an Advent collection of her hand-lettered artwork, I thought my part would be simply throwing together a few little devos to go with her art. I'd call it done and go on about my business.

But God.

He wasn't having any of that. He drew me into his Word and took me on a journey through Christmas past and glory future. There have been times when I had to walk away from my Bible and laptop to go sit on the floor, take a breath, and and warm the chill bumps. And occasionally, weep.

What you hold in your hands is the outcome of that journey. I have never been more in love with God's Word than I am after he has been so gracious to open my eyes to behold more of Jesus.

I pray your eyes are opened as well and you fall deeper into love with the Christ of Christmas, the Cross, and the Crown of glory.

There is something uniquely special about this part of God's story.

After you BEHOLD, you may never be the same again.

Watching and waiting with you,

Christi

We've created additional resources for you to take along for the journey at:

BEHOLDADVENT.COM:

- A YouTube playlist of Christmas hymns reflected in the subtitles of these chapters.
- A collection of art inspired by favorite lines of treasured hymns (corresponding to the chapter subtitles). Use these as note cards, display them in your home or office, or even send them to friends.
- A free schedule you can download to expand this book into a 24-day devotional journey.

We even have a prayer challenge
to take you into the New Year.
It's based on the truth you'll ponder in this book.

Go to Behold2018.com to sign up.

Before you begin ...

If you've been drawn to this Advent series,
you likely have accepted Christ as Savior.

But if not, please go to:
ChristiGee.com/hope
for more information on eternal life.

The promises described in this book
are only for those who know Jesus as LORD.

Behold

COME AND BEHOLD HIM

**"And the Word became flesh and dwelt among us,
and we *beheld* His glory,
the glory as of the only begotten of the Father,
full of grace and truth."
(John 1:14, NKJV)**

Christmas has a distinctive *look* unlike any other holiday we celebrate. It differs between cultures and families, but everyone knows what Christmas looks like to them. "Getting ready for Christmas" usually begins with the decorations that set the foundation for the look.

Christmas has a look. And the first message about Christmas was a call to *look* — or rather, *behold*. The angel told Mary:

"And ***behold***, you will conceive in your womb and bear a son, and you shall call his name Jesus."
(Luke 1:31)

However, *behold* goes beyond a simple look and often underscores the call to *see something new*. It is used in the New Testament "*when a thing is specified which is unexpected yet sure*" or seems "*impossible and yet occurs.*" In other places, it is the equivalent to observe or consider.[1] So although behold begins with *look*, it certainly doesn't end there. And neither does the message of Christmas. But it is a start.

Christmas is about looking.

The first response of the shepherds? *Go look.*
The reaction of the magi? *Seek and find.*
Even the old priest Simeon had been promised the blessing of seeing the Christ child before his dying breath.

So as you contemplate this Advent season, consider what has your focus. Where are you looking? What are you *beholding*?

1. Thayer's Greek Lexicon: biblehub.com/greek/2400.htm

If you're any version of normal, you likely need a little help adjusting your focus. The demands of the season so easily scoot in and crowd out the wonder of the meaning. We've heard and told the story a hundred times. We put up the manger scene and flip on the lights and move on to the next thing.

But what if we didn't this year?
What if we spent each day of Advent with a calling to BEHOLD?
One simple word:
...pondered before you even open your eyes.
...whispered in the middle of busy moments.
...written on cards; shared with family and friends.
...contemplated as you lay down each night.

Instead of a list of things to do, hear the invitation to BEHOLD what he has done. It will give you power over the "Christmas blues" that plague so many and set you up to avoid the "Christmas hangover" that often follows the season.

Choose this one word to be:
... a trigger to reflect on your blessings
... a response to deflect the stresses
... and a tool to log the "*God came near*" moments.

Let it be the inspiration to tune your heart to the awe-inspiring pulse of Christmas: *God.With.Us.* The Word became flesh. And dwelt. Among people. And what was the outcome for those who saw and came near? "We ***beheld*** his glory." Peter put it this way, "We were eyewitnesses of his majesty."[2]

The *impossible occurred* and the *unexpected was sure.* And because of Christmas, there was a Cross. And because of the Cross, there's now a Crown available to you and to me in Glory.

If you begin with BEHOLD, you'll naturally gravitate to glorify, praising his precious name. And that, dear friend, is where you'll truly see the Christ in Christmas.

Has it been a while since you've seen him? ***I mean really seen him?***

> If the troubles of this world occupy your mind, it's time for a redirected focus.
> If your prayers seem stale, you need a fresh infusion of his glory.
> And if you feel powerless to stand up to your

2. 2 Pet. 1:16

situation, maybe it's time to kneel before the Savior.

Ask him to help you see what you've been missing or show you things you never knew to seek.
Train your eyes on the fulfilled expectation of the first arrival and the glorious expectation of his second coming.
It's a game-changer and season-shifter.

Come and behold will lead to become.
Become less anxious and become more joyful.

When you behold, you'll be filled.
Filled with an awareness of his presence.

And if you've ***beheld***, you'll become more sensitive to being held. You'll be reminded you're not alone. It's not all up to you. You have a Savior who knows the troubles of this world and a God who loved you enough to send him to this cold earth.

So let's begin with BEHOLD and I promise you Christmas will take on a whole new *look*.

"Open my eyes, that I may *behold*
wondrous things out of your law."
(Ps. 119:18)

"For this reason I bow my knees
before the Father, from whom every family
in heaven and on earth is named,
that according to the riches of his glory
he may grant you to be strengthened
with power through his Spirit
in your inner being,
so that Christ may dwell
in your hearts through faith—
that you, being rooted and grounded in love,
may have strength to comprehend with all the saints
what is the breadth and length and height and depth,
and to know the love of Christ
that surpasses knowledge,
that you may be filled with all the fullness of God.
Now to him who is able to do
far more abundantly than all that we ask or think,
according to the power at work within us,
to him be glory in the church and in Christ Jesus
throughout all generations,
forever and ever. Amen."
(Eph. 3:14-21)

Prepare

LET EVERY HEART PREPARE HIM ROOM

**"*Behold,* I stand at the door and knock.
If anyone hears my voice and opens the door,
I will come in to him and eat with him,
and he with me."
(Rev. 3:20)**

Because all of my babies were induced, I knew when they would be born. On the night before we went to the hospital, I wrote each a letter.* I tried to prepare myself for the change that was about to wash over us, but there was no way to fathom the difference each one would make.

That first little bundle of blue came home and took over. And as he grew, my *stuff* diminished (or was moved to higher ground) and his *stuff* expanded. He filled my home and overflowed my heart.

Two years later, his baby sister did the same thing. The last child arrived just two weeks after we had moved into a new fixer-upper house. She didn't have nearly the *stuff* or preparation the other two had, but she had a mommy who knew how fast babyhood flies. I committed to making room and savoring moments and everything else could wait.

We often think of preparing for a child as buying baby equipment, painting the nursery, and stockpiling supplies.

As it turns out, the greatest need is to clear out and make room. Release our agenda. Resign our definition of perfect. Relinquish our own sleeping schedule, bathroom breaks, and dining plan. It becomes all about the baby.

So it is in preparing your heart's home for the Christ child. This time of year is naturally *full*. Modern day Christmas brings a host of extra activities to pile on top of normal responsibilities.

Advent won't happen if it's just another thing to do.

Pondering will be lost as your eyes dart down your list. And you'll miss out on this special season-induced opportunity to clear out and make room to receive and BEHOLD.

You may need to say "No" to some things on that list in order to say "Yes" to the gift God is offering. Christmas Advent is a unique opportunity that only comes once a year. Certainly, we can reflect on the Savior's birth any time, any day. But do we?

Getting ready for this baby is not just about buying gifts and throwing up lights but about acknowledging your poverty and exposing your dark spots. So do what you need to do to make room in your schedule. But even more importantly, take time to examine the rooms of your heart:

What longing is going unfulfilled by this world?
How often do you murmur, "If only ..."
Where does sin have a foothold?
Where is self-sufficiency occupying center stage?
Are you struggling for worth or weary of waiting?
What is stealing your peace and inflaming your fear?

You can probably identify with the little boy who prepared for his part in the Christmas play.
He was an angel who was supposed to deliver this one line: "It is I; don't be afraid!" He rehearsed with his grandma again and again, "It is I; don't be afraid."

But when the spotlight came on and blinded him, he froze. The stiff silence was broken with his whimper: *"It's me. And I'm scared."*

Most of our fears, stolen peace, and failure-centered feelings trace back to one thing: too much of me.

If you take a breath long enough to let the Holy Spirit make room, sweeping out the *I's*, discarding the *mine's*, and overwhelming the *me's*, your heart will be ready to receive and BEHOLD the gift of HIM.

It may not be comfortable, but it might be
God's greatest Christmas gift to you.

And if your Advent leaves your heart empty of self and full of Christ, it could usher in a New Year full of resolve with more room to accomplish his will.

**Full disclosure: I only wrote the first two their letters on the eve of their birth. The third got hers a year later. #LastChildProbs*

"Tell those who are invited, 'See, I have prepared my dinner, my oxen and my fat calves have been slaughtered, and everything is ready. Come to the wedding feast.'"
(Matt. 22:4)

Worship

FALL ON YOUR KNEES

"And the angel said to them,
'Fear not, for *behold,*
I bring you good news of great joy
that will be for all the people.'"
(Luke 2:10)

Can you imagine the angels watching God descend nine months before this night to live in Mary's womb?

Did they wonder what he was up to?

And then he finally reappeared as a baby and God gave one angel the privilege of announcing the news.

But as soon as that chosen one finished, the rest of them couldn't stand it any longer.

"And *suddenly* there was with the angel a multitude of the heavenly host praising God and saying, 'Glory to God in the highest, and on earth peace among those with whom he is pleased!'"
(Luke 2:13-14)

Church broke out in the sky.

After all, Christmas was the greatest "Call to Worship" in history. Mary's response was to worship. The magi left their oriental splendor to worship. The shepherds left their sheep to go see and then went away worshipping.

And the multitude of angels broke out into a full praise and worship session. However, note the specific word used to describe the *choir* — "host" — which means army. These weren't harp-playing, cloud-floating messengers "*bending near.*" They were a troop of warriors who came off the frontlines to join the worship service.

Can we press pause on that thought for a minute? Come with me back to the *real world*, as we often say when we're trying to put things in perspective.

Joseph and Mary were hanging out in a stable far from home with a brand-new baby. The heavenly host were hanging out in the sky giving glory when there were a *host* of ***real needs*** like clothing, food, and better shelter. And that's just for starters.

Didn't these warrior troops have battles to be fighting or important principalities to be guarding? At the very least, couldn't they have made a "to-do" or "to-buy" list for the shepherds so they wouldn't have arrived empty-handed? Come on, *let's be practical here.*

That's a facetious thought in the context of the Christmas story. But what about our day-to-day ***real lives*** when the *practical* needs mount?

We see this play out between Martha and Mary. Luke records that Martha was "distracted with much serving." He didn't say she was doing unnecessary things — these were probably good, *practical* ways she was ministering and putting the needs of others first. Jesus didn't rebuke her for serving, but he did note she was "*anxious and troubled about many things.*" On the other hand, Mary sat at Jesus' feet and he said she had chosen the "***good portion.***"[1]

The specific Greek word translated "good" in that statement has this definition: "*good whether it be seen to*

1. Luke 10:38-42

be so or not."[2] Isn't that one of our greatest challenges — determining priorities and what is a good use of our time, even when it's not easily discernible? In the middle of the holiday craziness, it's easy to discount the value of worship and sitting at Jesus' feet.

This is the thought to BEHOLD today.

Where and how will you make room to worship this season? Come in off the frontlines. Leave the to-do list on the table. Step away from the kitchen.
No, you can't shirk responsibilities, but you might have to decide to give less to others so you can give Jesus his rightful portion.

The creator of the universe
doesn't need anything from you,
but he knows how much you need to give.

If you're a parent, you've experienced this reality. You've unwrapped glitter-filled, glued-on, grubby macaroni art and celebrated it like it was a brick of gold. You need another art project to hang up like you need another hole in your head. But you know how much your children need to give back to you. So you let them and even encourage them to make

2. biblehub.com/greek/18.htm

more. You receive it with gladness, and they walk away with a full heart.

So it is with you.

You were created for worship. And if it goes unfulfilled, you're likely to find yourself like Martha, "*anxious and troubled.*" Worship ushers in peace and makes "*fear not*" possible. It changes where you look and reminds you who to trust.

Worship is both a response to — and a conduit for — joy. And it's liquid-plumber-gold for a clogged heart.

It's also God's gift of grace to you.

Take time today and make a plan for the coming days to worship. If the *heavenly host* can come off the frontlines to hang out in the sky, so can you.

Practice falling on your knees now. After all, it's where you're going to spend a great deal of eternity.

"…day and night they never cease to say,
'Holy, holy, holy, is the Lord God Almighty,
who was and is and is to come!'
And whenever the living creatures give glory and
honor and thanks to him who is seated on the
throne, who lives forever and ever, the twenty-four
elders fall down before him who is seated on the
throne and worship him who lives forever and ever.
They cast their crowns before the throne, saying,
'Worthy are you, our Lord and God,
to receive glory and honor and power,
for you created all things,
and by your will they existed and were created.'"
(Rev. 4:8-11)

Fulfilling

O HOLY NIGHT

"All this took place to fulfill what the Lord had spoken by the prophet: '*Behold,* the virgin shall conceive and bear a son, and they shall call his name Immanuel" (which means, God with us).'"
(Matt. 1:22-23)

Fulfill. The night God lay in a manger separated the age of promise from the age of fulfillment. There would be no more waiting for God to make good on his promise to send the Messiah. Heaven intersected earth and all of history was divided. The anticipation of the ages got its answer.

But prior to this night: "*long lay the world,*" as the song lyrics proclaim. When Gabriel announced the news to Mary, he referenced this prophecy:

"And the Lord God will give to him the throne of his father David, and he will reign over the house of Jacob forever, and of his kingdom there will be no end."
(Luke 1:32b–33)

That promise had been given to King David 1000 years before and repeated by Isaiah, who recorded a great volume of prophecies about the coming Messiah. In the final chapters, he delivered these words from God:

"I am the Lord; in its time I will hasten it."
(Isa. 60:22b)

The fulfillment of the promises depended directly on God, who has never been bound by time. He wasn't waiting on favorable circumstances or history to be on his side. No, he wrote, directed, and produced *his story*, er history.

The original Old Testament hearers of Isaiah's words were living in the messy middle between the "*already*" and the "*not yet.*" Their ancestors had been delivered from Egypt, received the Law, heard the prophets, and experienced the glory of God as it filled the Tabernacle. But the promised Savior had not come.

And he would not come for 700 years more. And get this — it was going to get worse for them before it ever got better. They still had Babylonian captivity in their future.

Think about the many centuries the promise went UNfulfilled. The Hebrews *Hall of Faith* ends by noting that NONE of those heroes received what was promised.[1]

So why is this worth contemplating today? What is here to BEHOLD?

You are also living in the messy middle between the "*already*" and the "*not yet.*" You've been delivered from eternal death, received the words of life, and his Spirit is tabernacled within you. But this world is not your home. And *favorable circumstances* are not God's focus; in fact, it might get worse before it gets better. God is writing a story with your life and it's all about his glory.

And often, you'll be called to wait; expectations and dreams might go unfulfilled. You're not wired to enjoy waiting. The flesh screams for answers in view and the enemy of souls is all too happy to plant seeds

1. Heb. 11:39

of disappointment. If those seeds grow into a perception that God has lost interest in your life, you might be tempted to cut your losses and give up on the promises.

But Christmas happened because
God always keeps his promises.

And that's the truth to BEHOLD today. Christmas says, "Don't let what didn't happen yesterday make you live like it couldn't happen today."

And furthermore, it reminds you that the best answers often arrive in the most unpredictable packages. Think about how unexpected was the event that satisfied the expectancy of a millennium.

The message of Christmas is a call to *keep believing, keep trusting, and keep serving.*

Paul ended his message to the Galatians with a charge of perseverance for the "*in between*" and a call to continued hope for the "*not yet.*" And then he told them what they should do while they waited:

"And let us not grow weary of doing good,
for in due season we will reap, if we do not give up.
So then, as we have opportunity, let us do good

to everyone, and especially to those
who are of the household of faith."
(Gal. 6:9-10)

If this season finds you weary or tired of waiting, focus today on how the timing of the first Christmas speaks to your soul.

Confess your struggle to God and ask him for fresh strength to keep going and keep believing.

And most importantly, ask him to guard your heart against growing cold or losing sight of his promise-keeping nature.

You are, after all,
living in the age of fulfillment.
This is a beautiful side of history to be on.

And one day, the story will be fulfilled
when Jesus returns to take you home.
The "*already*" will merge with the "*it's time*"
and you'll forget you ever had to wait.

"Let us hold unswervingly to the hope we profess, for he who promised is faithful. And let us consider how we may spur one another on toward love and good deeds."
(Heb. 10:23-24)

"But when the fullness of time had come, God sent forth his Son, born of woman, born under the law, to redeem those who were under the law, so that we might receive adoption as sons."
(Gal. 4:4-5)

Joy

A WEARY WORLD REJOICES

"… And *behold*, I am with you always,
to the end of the age."
(Matt. 28:20)

How December 25th came to be the date we celebrate Jesus' birth is steeped in politics and pagan festivals. But there's something about the timing that feels providential. Without this reason to BEHOLD something magnificent and promise-filled, we'd likely let the year-end reflections dictate our focus.

Time that slipped through our fingers.
Unfulfilled hopes and dreams.
Aspects of life that aren't like they used to be.
Mounting overwhelm.
More weary than wonderful.

But instead, because of Christmas we are invited to focus on Christ. We are reminded that this good news brought — and still brings — great joy.

Great. Joy.

Not happiness, but joy. Happiness shares the same English root with happenings. That root implies chance. Things that are out of your control. Fleeting. Changing. Perishable.

Happiness happens. But joy abides. One is contingent on circumstances; the other rises above them.

The circumstances that set the stage for the first Christmas were void of comfort and ease. The song expresses it well: *a weary world*. The people awaiting the promise lived in the margins, both politically and economically with diminishing influence, scarce resources, and often fearing for their lives.

It's into this darkness that the proclamation broke through. They weren't suddenly rich, safe, and in control. But when they received the good news, the age of indestructible joy was ushered in, despite unchanging circumstances.

Joy effervesces throughout the Christmas narrative. Consider that Matthew even says the magi "*rejoiced with great joy.*" Under normal circumstances, the editor in me would comment about the redundancy of that statement. But if there's one occasion worth a double dose of joy, it's the birth of the Christ child, Immanuel.

God with us.
This was why that night was the dawning
of unshakable, unchangeable,
permanent, and perpetual joy.

God came down to dwell with men. And before he left to return to heaven he made a promise. Jesus' words, "I am with you always, to the end of the age," are the **ongoing fulfillment of the promise of *Immanuel.***

Today, take an intermission from all of the weary-inducing demands of the season to BEHOLD this truth:

Immanuel resides in you.

When the Son went back to heaven, the Spirit remained. You are a walking Christmas story if you've received him as Savior.

God with us was not just for the Holy night; it's for the manic Monday, weary Wednesday, and saturated Saturday.

Joy does not manifest because of what is going on around us but is produced because the Holy Spirit takes control of what is inside of us. In fact, Scripture often juxtaposes joy with sorrow and trials.

One of the most poignant for us to consider today is found in Jesus' final words to his disciples before going to the cross. There in the upper room, he compared the relationship of worldly sorrow and supernatural joy to a woman giving birth, pointing out the mother never remembers the anguish once the joy is delivered.[1]

Sorrow will not last.
And in the middle of a broken world,
we have unbreakable joy.

Jesus' words on sorrow and joy end with a well-known declaration perfect for BEHOLDING today:

"In the world you will have tribulation.
But take heart; I have overcome the world."
(John 16:33)

1. John 16:20-22

The reason the weary world doesn't get the final say is because it has been overcome.

And the overcomer, joy-giver, peace-sustainer now resides in your heart.

Reflect on that truth like it was a brand new gift.
BEHOLD it close and proclaim it with all the passion you can muster.
Turn up the volume on "Joy to the World" and put it on repeat.
Ask the Spirit to bring joy deep from within and let it rise up in your soul, washing over your weary whimpers with resounding praise.

Celebrate *God with us* inside of you and the truth that one day you will live inside the home he is preparing.

BEHOLD!

He came.

He abides.

He comes.

"Sing and rejoice, O daughter of Zion, for *behold*, I come and I will dwell in your midst, declares the Lord."
(Zech. 2:10)

"And I heard a loud voice from the throne saying, "*Behold*, the dwelling place of God is with man. He will dwell with them, and they will be his people, and God himself will be with them as their God."
(Rev. 21:3)

"So also you have sorrow now, but I will see you again, and your hearts will rejoice, and no one will take your joy from you."
(John 16:20-22)

Hope

A THRILL OF HOPE

"*Behold*, the eye of the Lord
is on those who fear him,
on those who hope in his steadfast love."
(Ps. 33:18)

Our lives pivot on and revolve around the hinge pin of hope. Every decision, response, and relationship is fueled by it. Happiness is hope fulfilled and sadness is hope destroyed.

There are almost 200 instances of the word "*hope*" in the Bible translated from about ten different Greek and Hebrew root words. Most of those roots share one commonality: *expectancy, expectation, waiting expectantly.* They project the source of trust and confidence, and most of them have a positive connotation. However, right before today's opening verse, the word is used to convey the negative:

"The war horse is a *false hope* for salvation, and by its great might it cannot rescue."
(Ps. 33:17)

The phrase "*false hope*" stems from a Hebrew word meaning disappointment or deception, and that word is used throughout the Old Testament far more times than the words for true hope. That's interesting when you consider our tendency to look for hope in all the wrong places and all the counterfeit things.

True, living, blessed, soul-anchoring hope has a name —Jesus. You know this. You profess this. But do you live like you believe this?

Here's a test. Complete this sentence: "If only I had ________, then my life would be full, good, etc." Anything that fits into that blank is *false hope*.

False hope is the root of hopelessness. Hope always has an object and/or expectation, and if you place anything or anyone in that role other than Jesus, you are sure to be disappointed. You will never experience hope as God intends until your life is void of all other sources of false hope.

So here's the good news:

*Hopelessness is often the ground
into which true hope can take root.*

Isaiah 59-60 illustrates this brilliantly. The last third of Isaiah was written as a foretelling of the future, both for the remnant who would return from captivity in the sixth century B.C. and the rest of history who would read Isaiah's inspired words until Jesus returns.

In the post-exilic period, both Jerusalem and the Jews were a mess. In chapter 59 Isaiah describes the depth of their sin and the people's recognition of the weight of their transgressions. They are completely out of options and have totally lost their way, "groping for the wall like the blind, growling like bears, hoping for justice but finding salvation is far away."

Consider this one sentence summary:

"We hope for light, and *behold*, darkness,
and for brightness, but we walk in gloom."
(Isa. 59:9b)

It is onto this dark stage of complete hopelessness that the star of the story appears. Yahweh takes over, displaying the power of a fully equipped warrior and interceding for his people. From there, chapter 60 launches into a description of future glory.

The message of this passage is also the underlying theme of the entire biblical narrative:

Hope forfeited. Hope restored. Hope fulfilled.

This is the truth to BEHOLD and the message to contemplate. There's only one who can be counted on to fulfill expectations; everything but Jesus will eventually disappoint.

When you realize it is hopeless to hope in anybody else, then the doorway to real hope in your life will open. It's often in your darkest moments that the true objects of your hope are revealed. But when you get to the end of yourself and relinquish all your expectations of others and perfect circumstances, then you are prepared to give the true source its rightful place.

Open up the dark corners of your heart and call out any imposters who are posing as an expectation of hope. Rebuke the false hope. Restore the true hope.

Hope thrills only
when its only object is Jesus.

Hope invaded our world on Christmas night, walking onto center stage and launching Act 2 of the great story. And one day, Christ will return to complete the narrative. The word *hope* is noticeably absent from the book of Revelation.

That's because there will come a day when *expectancy, expectation, and waiting expectantly* will no longer be necessary.

"According to his great mercy, he has caused us to be born again to a living hope through the resurrection of Jesus Christ from the dead." (1 Pet. 1:3)

"… waiting for our blessed hope, the appearing of the glory of our great God and Savior Jesus Christ." (Titus 2:13)

"This hope we have as an anchor of the soul, a hope both sure and steadfast and one which enters within the veil, where Jesus has entered as a forerunner for us …" (Heb. 6:19-20a, NASB)

"… having the eyes of your hearts enlightened, that you may know what is the hope to which he has called you, what are the riches of his glorious inheritance in the saints …" (Eph. 1:18)

"… and hope does not disappoint, because the love of God has been poured out within our hearts through the Holy Spirit who was given to us." (Rom. 5:5)

"For in this hope we were saved. Now hope that is seen is not hope. For who hopes for what he sees?" (Rom. 8:24)

"May the God of hope fill you with all joy and peace in believing, so that by the power of the Holy Spirit you may abound in hope." (Rom. 15:13)

Dawning

WITH THE DAWN OF REDEEMING GRACE

"The next day he saw Jesus
coming toward him, and said,
"*Behold*, the Lamb of God,
who takes away the sin of the world!"
(John 1:29)

Did you know there are multiple definitions of dawn? Astronomical dawn appears to be the most common and is defined as *18 degrees below the horizon.*[1] At this point, the rays of light can't be distinguished, but they are there, permeating the upper atmosphere.

So what we normally consider as still being night is actually not. Even before the sun rises above the horizon the darkness is fading, although it may not be perceptible to the human eye.

1. https://www.timeanddate.com/astronomy/dawn.html

To an untrained observer, it might appear that the light is weak, unable to fully conquer the darkness at that moment. But in actuality, all the power of the light is in full measure; the timing simply hasn't arrived for twilight to break.

So it must have been as Mary carried the redeemer of all mankind in her womb. The dark and weary world thought it was still night. Little did they know it was only *18 degrees below horizon*. The SON might not have been distinguished, but the Kingdom of God was at hand.

The birth of Christ was the dawning of redemption.

And although that baby in the manger appeared helpless, that was an illusion. Already the darkness was weakening.

What the cradle started the Cross finished.

The dawning of redemption culminated in the Redeemer paying the price for redeeming mankind with his life. And what happened on that day when the sun was at its highest point in the sky? Darkness fell over the whole land for three hours.[2]

2. Matt. 27:45-46

It might have appeared the darkness had overcome the light. The one whose life was the Light of men cried out, "Into your hands, I commit my spirit." When the darkness was finished, Jesus breathed his last. The author of life was placed in a tomb. But what looked like night was only an illusion. This was, after all, why the Son left the presence of the Father and the glory of heaven.

From the moment he took his first baby steps
in Joseph's carpentry shop,
he was headed toward the nails of Calvary.

John chose not to mention Jesus' birth, instead taking us straight into the reason for the Incarnation. The Word became flesh and dwelt among us so that he could give his flesh to take away the sin of the world. He lived a perfect life and died a sinner's death. And John emphasizes the ultimate outcome of that sacrifice:

"For from his fullness
we have all received, grace upon grace."
(John 1:16)

Grace upon grace.

The dawn of redeeming grace on Christmas night was from the beginning a preparation for the grace upon grace fulfilled on Good Friday.

The holiday song declares, “Don’t save it all for Christmas day… “ Today, the message to consider goes more like this, “Don’t wait until Easter to BEHOLD the cross.”

Let this day of Advent draw you into
a fresh view of Christ’s redeeming grace.

Contemplate the journey from the worn wood of a manager to the splintered wood of the cross.
Behold the Lamb of God whom shepherds first saw.
Cradle in your heart the Savior who took away your sins.
Schedule an early morning to watch the sunrise. Peer out into the darkness in the moments before the rays appear and remember what you learned today about dawn. You don’t have to wait until Easter morning to attend a sunrise service.

"So they departed quickly from the tomb with fear and great joy, and ran to tell his disciples. And *behold*, Jesus met them and said, "Greetings!" And they came up and took hold of his feet and worshiped him."
(Matt. 28:8-9)

"No longer will there be anything accursed, but the throne of God and of the Lamb will be in it, and his servants will worship him. They will see his face, and his name will be on their foreheads. And night will be no more. They will need no light of lamp or sun, for the Lord God will be their light, and they will reign forever and ever."
(Rev. 22:3-5)

Looking

LIGHT AND LIFE TO ALL HE BRINGS

"... And *behold*, the star that they had seen when it rose went before them until it came to rest over the place where the child was." (Matt. 2:9)

The only foretelling of the star and the first representation of Jesus as light were given to unlikely walk-ons to the stage of history. The new star led a pagan, priestly tribe of people from the Orient to find the child. The history that paints our picture of the magi is fascinating, but at their core they were occultist astrologers with a heritage of ruling over captive Israel.[1] Furthermore, the only prophecy recorded about the new star was given through another gentile enemy of God's people, Balaam.[2]

1. gty.org/library/sermons-library/2182/who-were-the-wise-men
2. Num. 24:17

Scripture is full of references to Jesus as light, but when the author of life broke through the darkness a second time, those who worshiped the night were the ones to behold the star. *They were looking.*

Humanity is drawn to light.

Whenever tragedy or terrorism strikes, what's the response? Hold a candlelight vigil. Even those who are held captive by darkened hearts instinctively gravitate toward symbols that proclaim there's something more powerful than the darkness.

As a believer, you carry that power within. You've been given the light and commanded to let it shine before others so that when they behold Christ in you, they will give glory to the Father.

But I know it's not always easy. At times, the darkness can feel closer and stronger than the light. How long has it been since the last report of terrorism, heart-wrenching catastrophe, or insidious evil act? Not long, right?

We need the message of Christmas more than ever:
God hasn't left us in the dark.
He did something.

He didn't sit silent on the sidelines.
He broke through. Light came into the world.
And the darkness did not … has not … will not … overcome it.
God has never stopped being sovereign over all.

The *first* time he broke the darkness, he separated it with light he created from nothing. The *second* time he broke through to offer darkened hearts eternal light. The one who took on flesh is the one who gave Adam his. And the one for whom that star shone is the one who spoke the galaxies into existence.

Dear one, there is no darkness that the author of light and life cannot overcome. This is a crucial truth to BEHOLD today, both for your strength to endure and your courage to testify.

You simply cannot keep your light hidden under a bushel.

There's a pagan world consumed by the night.
Some are looking for something more and this holiday season may have softened their hearts to be ready to receive the gift they didn't know to ask for.

Some will choose to remain captive to the enemy, running from the message and embracing the darkness.[3]

And some who are enemies of God may even choose to become an enemy of God's people. And that includes you.

You don't have to know who is who.

You only have to carry your candle into the night, recalling that greater is he that is in you than he that is in the world.

Reflect today on the joy of your salvation and ask God to open doors and direct your eyes to find the opportunities to spread his joy this season.

BEHOLD the call of the Gospel and the Great Commission.

Speak life. Share Jesus. Shine light.

Be bold. Take heart. Have courage.

Because there will be a ***third*** breakthrough and then it will be too late. One day the sky will be filled with another new light — the bright and Morning Star.

May we not be guilty of having failed to lead anyone *who was looking* to find the Christ.

3. John 3:19

"In him was life, and the life was the light of men. The light shines in the darkness, and the darkness has not overcome it."
(John 1:4–5)

"You are the light of the world. A city set on a hill cannot be hidden. Nor do people light a lamp and put it under a basket, but on a stand, and it gives light to all in the house. In the same way, let your light shine before others, so that they may see your good works and give glory to your Father who is in heaven."
(Matt. 5:14–16)

"Little children, you are from God and have overcome them, for he who is in you is greater than he who is in the world."
(1 John 4:4)

"Again Jesus spoke to them, saying, 'I am the light of the world. Whoever follows me will not walk in darkness, but will have the light of life.'"
(John 8:12)

Redeemed

THE SOUL FELT ITS WORTH

"*Behold*, you are beautiful, my love,
***behold*, you are beautiful!"**
(Song of Solomon 4:1)

The book of Ruth opens with famine, death, emptiness, hopelessness, and bitterness, just to name a few. Ruth was empty-handed, disgraced by her position, and despised for her race. She had no worth and nothing to offer. Naomi, her mother-in-law, spoke without hesitation of the hand of the Lord being against her. That's all in chapter 1. But turn the page and behold chapter 2. Onto this scene enters the one who will eventually become the kinsman-redeemer, Boaz.

"And *behold*, Boaz came from Bethlehem. And he said to the reapers, 'The Lord be with you!' …"
(Ruth 2:4)

And by chapter 4, life has followed death; fullness has replaced emptiness; the future holds hope instead of despair.

And the difference?

The redeemer.

A destitute gentile from the cursed Moabite nation ended up in the Christmas story because she was grafted into the line of the Messiah. The worthless was considered worthy and the barren became a bride. All because God provided a wealthy Jewish redeemer.

Through the prophet Isaiah, God announced his plans to provide a Redeemer for all the unworthy and used the metaphor of a widow to describe the ones to whom he was coming.

"For your Maker is your husband,
the Lord of hosts is his name;
and the Holy One of Israel is your Redeemer,
the God of the whole earth he is called.
For the Lord has called you like a wife deserted and
grieved in spirit, like a wife of youth
when she is cast off …"
(Isa. 54:5-6)

In the verses before these, Isaiah describes the widowed people as full of shame, disgrace, and reproach; because of the Redeemer, that all will change.

There are two Hebrew words for "*redeem.*" Both convey the idea of rescue, but they each have different primary meanings. The one we often think of in context of the Gospel narrative is *padah*, which means to exchange a substitute or pay a ransom.

However, Isaiah prophesied primarily with the other Hebrew word, *gaal* — the same one used throughout the book of Ruth. This version of redeem or redeemer has its roots in the kinsman's protection. Isaiah's focus was on God's intent to rescue his people from their captivity and cultivate the conditions for their fidelity to flourish.

Isn't this beautiful
in light of the wedding imagery?

Just as Ruth came to Boaz empty-handed and disgraced, so you come to Christ with nothing but filthy rags and loads of debt. The bridegroom both pays your ransom and redeems your worth, offering his robe of righteousness. He covers you with the white gown, cradles your face, and whispers, "You are my beloved. And you are beautiful."

And then your soul receives the worth
ascribed to an heir of the King.

Life follows death. Fullness replaces emptiness. The future holds hope instead of despair. *What a difference the Redeeemer makes.*

Today, BEHOLD the difference the Redeemer makes in your life. Flip this truth around in your heart like you would a peppermint on your tongue. Savor and let it linger. And then, go forward in his beauty.

Walk like you are cherished
by the perfect bridegroom.
Wait for him like a bride at the back of the church.
Go ahead and live like you are loved.

Throw open the closet doors
and put on his robe of righteousness.
White looks good on you, after all.

"… My soul shall exult in my God, for he has clothed me with the garments of salvation; he has covered me with the robe of righteousness, as a bridegroom decks himself like a priest with a beautiful headdress, and as a bride adorns herself with her jewels."
(Isa. 61:10)

"… The marriage of the Lamb has come, and his Bride has made herself ready; it was granted her to clothe herself with fine linen, bright and pure — for the fine linen is the righteous deeds of the saints."
(Rev. 19:6–8)

"But when the goodness and loving kindness of God our Savior appeared, he saved us, not because of works done by us in righteousness, but according to his own mercy, by the washing of regeneration and renewal of the Holy Spirit, whom he poured out on us richly through Jesus Christ our Savior, so that being justified by his grace we might become heirs according to the hope of eternal life."
(Titus 3:4–7)

Overshadowed

MARY DID YOU KNOW ...

"And Mary said,
'*Behold*, I am the servant of the Lord;
let it be to me according to your word.'"
(Luke 1:38)

There are a few quotes about motherhood that cause me to pause when I consider them in light of Mary as a mommy.

"For the hand that rocks the cradle is the hand that rules the world." ~ William Ross Wallace
But what if the one in the cradle already rules the world?

"Sooner or later we all quote our mothers." ~ Bern Williams
Is there anything Jesus said that is rooted in his mom's advice?

And finally, this one:
"Making the decision to have a child …
is to decide forever to have your heart go walking
around outside your body. "
~ Elizabeth Stone

That one gets me; I know the reality of that statement fully. Watching my grown children launch is some of the toughest parenting I've done because I have very little say on where those pieces of my heart go and what they encounter and endure. To think of Mary watching that piece of her heart go to the cross sends chills up my spine.

There's much we don't know or can't fathom about Mary, but what we do know about her speaks volumes and *offers questions back to us for our own surrendered lives.* Consider this paraphrased version of her conversation with Gabriel:[1]

> Gabe: "Hey there! This is your lucky day. God is with you."
>
> Mary (to herself): "Who is this stranger and how did he get in my room? Who says that to a girl they don't even know?"

1. Luke 1:26-38

Gabe: "It's all good. Don't be scared. Look, you're going to have a baby boy named Jesus. He will have a lot of names, actually. One of those will be Son of the Most High."
"But wait! There's more!"
"He will be the fulfiller of that prophecy you've heard about all your life — the one your people have waited almost 1000 years to see come true."

Mary: "How? I am a virgin."

Gabe: "God's power through his Spirit will overshadow you. Thus, this child will be both holy and the Son of God."
"But wait! There's more!"
"Your old barren cousin Elizabeth is already in her third trimester, and it's a boy also! For nothing will be impossible with God."

Mary: "Alrighty then."

When presented with the impossible and unimaginable, Mary simply asked, "How?"

The answer was still unfathomable, but long before her son prayed, "*Not my will, but yours*" she declared, "*Let it be to me according to your word.*"

She allowed both her womb and her world to be overshadowed by the Most High. And just like that, all her little girl dreams of her ideal future vanished.

> For the rest of her life, some might look at her as "*that kind of girl.*"
> She would spend years on the run, looking over her shoulder wondering if the stranger was a danger to her baby.
> Her heart didn't just walk around on the outside of her body; it was pierced by a sword.[2]

That's the story she was asked to step into. But her first response — when all she knew was that her agenda had been overruled — was worship. Her soul rejoiced. Obedience produced joy, and submission opened the door to a purpose far beyond her imagination. If we could talk to her now, we'd hear her say, *"Jesus was worth it."*

The story of Christmas is a call to be overshadowed.

It rises up, stares us in the face, and interrogates our hearts:

> "Will you believe, even when it seems impossible?"

2. Luke 2:35; John 19:25, 34

> "Will you rejoice, even when life looks nothing like you imagined?"
> "Will you endure, even if the cost is high?"

Today, the questions for you to BEHOLD are these:

> What plan, person, or dream are you holding in higher esteem than Jesus?
> Where are you screaming *Thy will be changed* instead of *Thy will be done*?
> How is your joy being compromised because of failure to submit?

Take your answers to the Lord in prayer and ask him to help you release your grip. After all, the call to discipleship is an invitation to lay down our dreams and pick up a cross. For the rest of our lives, we make course adjustments — and count it all joy.

Not because it is easy
but because Jesus is worth it.

"Blessed is she who believed, for there will be a completion to those things which were told her by the Lord.

And Mary said,

'My soul magnifies the Lord,
    and my spirit rejoices in God my Savior,
for he has looked on the humble estate of his servant.
    For *behold*, from now on all generations will call me blessed;
for he who is mighty has done great things for me,
    and holy is his name.'"
(Luke 1:45-49)

Delivered

CHAINS HE SHALL BREAK

"*Behold*, the Lord's hand is not so short that it cannot save; Nor is His ear so dull that it cannot hear." (Isa. 59:1, NASB)

Have you ever pondered the poetic irony God wove into his story by sending Joseph and Mary into the safety of Egypt to protect their — his — firstborn?[1]

Contemplate with me …

Centuries earlier, an Egyptian Pharaoh had decreed death for all the Hebrew infant boys. God providentially arranged for baby Moses to live, as he was the Lord's chosen one to deliver his people from slavery. When the timing was right, God used Moses to proclaim to Pharaoh, "Let my people go." The final

1. Matt. 2:13-24

deliverance for the Israelites came after all of Egypt lost their firstborn sons. God's people were saved from the death angel because they obeyed the Passover instructions, slaughtering an unblemished lamb and placing its blood on their wooden doorposts.[2] Almost 1500 years later, Joseph and Mary's firstborn and God's perfect Lamb would spill his blood on a splintered cross so that all people could be saved from eternal death.

Add rich foreshadowing to that poetic irony, right? Let's continue with the story because there's something profound tucked in this narrative for our lives today.

Once the Israelites were freed from Egyptian bondage and marching toward the Promised Land, they *still* needed saving. Caught between an impassible sea and the Egyptian enemy hot on their heels, their first reaction was despair.

They cried out again, as they had cried out while still enslaved. Exodus chapter 2 tells us the first time *God heard, God saw, and God knew*. This time, Scripture records God told them:

2. Ex. 1-12

"Do not be afraid.
Stand still, and see the salvation of the Lord,
which He will accomplish for you today. …
The Lord will fight for you,
and you shall hold your peace."
(Ex. 14:13-14, NKJV)

As it turned out, their chain-breaking, prison-shaking God was also a way-making sea-divider.

In the middle of their story between freedom from shackles and the promise of a land to call their own, we find the truth to BEHOLD for today. Christmas started what the Cross finished, but it won't be complete until we wear the Crown.

Salvation is past, present, and future.

You have been saved from the power and penalty of sin, but you are not yet free from its presence. Just because you're no longer a slave to sin doesn't mean you won't struggle with it. And the enemy will not give up stalking your soul until he is bound in his own eternal chains. Consider Paul's words in Romans 7. He had already been delivered from eternal death, but here he sounds like a man caught in no man's land:

"So I find it to be a law that when I want to do right, evil lies close at hand. For I delight in the law of God, in my inner being, but I see in my members another law waging war against the law of my mind and making me *captive* to the law of sin that dwells in my members. Wretched man that I am! Who will *deliver* me from this body of death?"
(Rom. 7: 21-24)

Thankfully, he goes on to reveal the supernatural answer to the fleshly struggle — the Holy Spirit. Whereas the Spirit was mentioned only one time in the letter up to this point, chapter 8 overflows with references, including the truth that the Spirit is the one who grants us strength for victory over our unredeemed flesh.

The message of Christmas is not just about God coming to earth and taking on flesh.

It's about the ongoing power over flesh
because God's Spirit remained
after God's Son returned to heaven.

Dear one, BEHOLD this promise:
You carry the power of the chain-breaking deliverer within you. As you journey toward the Promised

Land, you won't be sinless — but you are empowered to sin less. If you feel hemmed in by the enemy or face a seemingly impossible situation, cry out to your way-making Savior. Ask him to show you the way of escape from the temptation you face. *He hears, he sees, and he knows.*

He not only delivered you from the enemy's shackles, he gave you himself to sanctify and continually rescue you from the enemy's chase and the flesh's carnal nature.

Stand still, and see the salvation of the Lord,
which He will accomplish for you today.

"No temptation has overtaken you that is not common to man. God is faithful, and he will not let you be tempted beyond your ability, but with the temptation he will also provide the way of escape, that you may be able to endure it."
(1 Cor. 10:13)

Interceding

WHAT CHILD IS THIS? THIS. THIS IS CHRIST THE KING

"Pilate said to them, '*Behold* the man!'"
(John 19:5)
"… [Pilate] said to the Jews, "*Behold* your King!"
(John 19:14)

In the span of ten verses, John used Pilate's own words to encapsulate the enigma of all eternity: *God as man.* The King of all creation held captive in human flesh.

The infinite, eternal One was once only minutes old.

And then he was a toddler.

And then a teen.

And from there …

a teacher whose students never understood.
a preacher whose audience stabbed him in the back.
a friend whose comrades betrayed him at his darkest hour.
a single who never married.

The humanity of the Son is a pivotal teaching, yet the theology is rarely pondered except on Christmas and Easter. So let's take advantage of Advent to BEHOLD this truth and drink deeply from the well it offers.

Why does it matter that God took on flesh — that he was 100 percent God and 100 percent man? Beyond the implications of salvation and the perfect sacrifice, the humanity of Christ testifies:

"For we do not have a High Priest who cannot sympathize with our weaknesses, but was in all points tempted as we are, yet without sin."
(Heb. 4:15, NKJV)

I used to have a little trouble fully responding to this doctrine. It felt like one of those ideas so lofty it couldn't reach earth to walk with me. I accepted it as inspired truth; I just didn't know how to let it affect my daily response.

My mind argued back,
"Yes. But.He.Was.God. Hellooooo!"
(point heavenward) "Trinity."
(point inward) "Not Trinity."

Maybe you can relate?

It's as if the writer of Hebrews anticipated our argument because he went on to unpack this idea. In chapter 5 he described the qualifications for high priesthood under the Levitical system. The one that matters to us today is in verse 2, where he noted that a high priest had to be humanly sympathetic and beset with weakness.

Beset with weakness. **But how can that be fulfilled in Jesus?** Well, the short answer is the Garden of Gethsemane. In order to show that Jesus was beset with weakness, the Hebrews author referenced the excruciating, soul-crushing point in time when Jesus cried aloud, asking God to find another way.[1] He was distressed, exhausted, and full of so much anxiety that his capillaries burst, causing him to sweat blood.[2]

1. Heb. 5:7-8 | With thanks to Matt Chandler and the Village Church for the sermons on Hebrews that helped me better understand this connection. You can find the series here: tvcresources.net/resource-library/series-index/hebrews
2. Matt. 26; Luke 22

The Hebrews author connected the dots for us, pointing out that in that moment, Jesus felt the full weight that accompanies sin. All the shame. All the guilt. All the despair. The entire force of what we feel from our own failures began to crush him. And he wanted to escape.

So yes.
He didn't just save you;
he "gets you."

He knows how overwhelmed you feel about that sin you can't conquer. He understands how shame follows you around like a dark cloud and guilt nips at your heels. He looks at your deepest desperation and sympathizes.

He's not in heaven shaking his head and tapping his foot while shouting, "When are you going to figure this out? I swear, one more time and I'm done with you. You can help yourself out of this one."

No. In fact, it's just the opposite. Because the King who sits at the right hand of the Father interceding for us has faced what we face, the Hebrews author declared:

"Let us therefore come boldly to the throne of grace, that we may obtain mercy and find grace to help in time of need."
(Heb. 4:16, NKJV)

You don't have to figure it out yourself, wondering if he's got an ounce of patience left. Don't run and hide; throw yourself boldly at his mercy and ask him for the help you need.

That's what he's there for.
That's what he came for.

Just hours before Pilate mocked him as both man and king, Jesus responded to his question:

"You say correctly that I am a king. For this I have been born, and for this I have come into the world, to testify to the truth."
(John 18:37, NASB)

The King on the throne of grace was once
the child in a manger,
the man in the garden,
and the sinless sacrifice on the cross.

He was born to die.
But he lived to understand your weakness.

HE KNOWS HOW SCARY IT IS TO BE YOU.

BEHOLD that reality today.
Let it sink in deeply and draw you into a full awareness of his power, his presence, and his prayer.

Unlike his own sleepy friends in the garden, he's always up to pray for you.

"Therefore He is also able to save to the uttermost those who come to God through Him, since He always lives to make intercession for them."
(Heb. 7:25, NKJV)

Coming

GLORIA IN EXCELSIS DEO

**"*Behold,* he is coming with the clouds,
and every eye will see him ..."
(Rev. 1:7)**

The first time Jesus came to earth, many missed him. Even those who looked him in the face didn't see him for who he was.

That won't happen the next time he comes.

Every eye will BEHOLD him, and it won't be just the heavenly host singing his praises. ALL glory will be given to him in the highest.

Advent means arrival. Here at this season, we remember the first arrival and remind ourselves to hold fast to the promise of the second coming.

We've mentioned that here in the messy middle we are surrounded by a creation that groans and people who disappoint. But Jesus promised it won't be like this forever. Despair won't hold us for ransom; chaos won't always be our companion; discouragement doesn't get the final word.

In the upper room, Jesus looked his disciples in the eyes before he went to the cross and in essence said, "Trust me. I will never give up on you; don't give up on me." The disciples couldn't comprehend any of it, but Jesus knew the greatest hope for their darkest hours lay in his promise that he was coming back.[1]

I'm so thankful God wanted us to know what Christ said in those final hours because I believe John's record is one of the most insightful looks into the heart of Christ in all of Scripture.

Just hours before he was to experience complete abandonment, the despair of all eternity, and excruciating torment, his friends were first and foremost on his mind. Filled with compassion, he focused on consoling them, "Let not YOUR heart be troubled." He went on to remind them he had always kept his promises, asking them to continue to trust

1. John 14

him before they got the next answer. He knew the waiting would seem endless and they'd be tempted to give in to despair. He affirmed his love, offered his peace, and gave them a reason to hold onto hope.

And then he used a metaphor they understood but sometimes is lost on us. He implanted a picture in their minds that would carry them through the rest of their lives.

> "In my Father's house are many rooms;
> if it were not so, I would have told you;
> for I go to prepare a place for you."
> (John 14:2)

When a first-century Jewish boy and girl wanted to get married, the engagement process began with a negotiation. The future groom approached the girl's father for permission and if the father agreed, the next step was to settle on a price — often very costly. Once the father was satisfied with the payment terms he poured a glass of wine and drank to symbolize his acceptance.

Once the father accepted the offer, he handed the drink to the groom. The groom took the cup and by drinking, pledged his oath to pay for the bride. From there, the covenant was established and the two were committed to each other forever.

And then the groom left.

He went back to his father's house to build a room for his bride. While he prepared the home, the bride stayed with her family. She readied herself for him, waiting expectantly and never thinking for a moment that he might not come again.

His return was usually at night so the bright lights that went before him first announced his arrival. Once identified, his presence was heralded throughout the city with trumpets and shouts of, *"He is coming! He is coming!"*

That night in the upper room Jesus used the same present tense verb with his disciples as John recorded in Revelation: "*I am coming.*"

The truth to BEHOLD both today and as you go forward from here is this: *He is coming.*

As you walk between the "*already*" and "*not yet,*" let this infuse your perspective and quell your fears. It's the source of your unbreakable joy and the reason hope thrills your soul.

Christmas affirmed God always keeps his promises; Easter reminds us it's often darkest before the dawn. In the middle of hopelessness, the baby arrived and the Savior arose, and one day that new and glorious morn will never give way to darkness again.

Church will break out in the sky one more time and all humanity will see his light.

The presence of sin will be removed from your life as every last chain is broken and the deliverance is complete.

The Redeemer-bridegroom will call you forward from the back of the church and take you before the throne of grace. You won't need an intercessor because you'll be living in the presence of a satisfied King.

You will be overshadowed by his glory as you exchange your cross for a crown and fall to your knees proclaiming, "*Worthy is the Lamb.*"

BEHOLD, He. Is. Coming.

So never stop looking.

On the day when he returns to take you home to glory, you'll know it was worth the wait.

“Let not your hearts be troubled.
Believe in God; believe also in me …
I will come again and will take you to myself,
that where I am you may be also …
I will not leave you as orphans;
I will come to you …
Peace I leave with you; my peace I give to you.
Not as the world gives do I give to you.
Let not your hearts be troubled,
neither let them be afraid …

And behold, I am coming soon …
Behold, I am coming soon …
Surely I am coming soon.”

Amen. Come, Lord Jesus!
(John 14:1, 3, 18, 27; Rev. 22:7, 12, 20)

Additional Advent materials at:
BeholdAdvent.com

Join the prayer challenge based on the reflections in this book and keep the journey going:
Behold2018.com

About the Author

CHRISTI GEE

Making Life and Words Count

...

Christi Gee is a listener, speaker, writer, and forever student of God's Word.

She began teaching the Bible while she was still a teen. Through the decades, she led children's ministries and wrote church and Christian school curriculum on subjects such as worldview, apologetics, and chronological scope and sequences.

While still working as a marketing director at Liberty University, she began blogging and now reaches thousands each week through her work at ChristiGee.com.

Through the years, her professional career in marketing and her volunteer activities in ministry always took a back seat to her highest calling: raising her three children.

Now that they are launched and the nest is empty, she has begun branching out, opening doors to find the next thing.

Although Texans for over four decades, she and her husband, Eddie, now live on the East Coast.

Find out more about her speaking or marketing consulting services here: christigee.com/work-with-me/

Connect with her in these places:

Facebook: @ChristiGeeDotCom
Instagram: @ChristiLGee
Twitter: @ChristiLGee

Revival

6 Steps to Reviving Your Heart and Rebuilding Your Prayer Life

Continue your journey
with this author's book on prayer:
Revival

Download a sample chapter at RevivalPray.com

Find it on Amazon in ebook or paperback.

Revival
6 STEPS TO REVIVING YOUR HEART
AND REBUILDING YOUR PRAYER LIFE
CHRISTI GEE

Prayer is powerful.
And praying with purpose — grounded in truth from God's Word — will result in renewal, revival, and regaining ground the enemy has stolen.

Revival: 6 Steps to Reviving Your Heart and Rebuilding Your Prayer Life began as a prayer challenge and became a lifeline for many.

The steps follow a construction analogy, with the goal of helping you rebuild your prayer life and evict any enemy squatters from your heart.

If you need revival in your life,
this prayer journey is for you.

Made in the USA
Middletown, DE
03 November 2018